EFFECTIVE CLASSROOM COMMUNICATION

Pocketbook

Richard Churches

Cartoons:
Phil Hailstone

Published by:

Teachers' Pocketbooks
Laurel House, Station Approach,
Alresford, Hampshire SO24 9JH, UK
Tel: +44 (0)1962 735573
Fax: +44 (0)1962 733637
E-mail: sales@teacherspocketbooks.co.uk
Website: www.teacherspocketbooks.co.uk

*Teachers' Pocketbooks is an imprint of
Management Pocketbooks Ltd.*

Series editor – Linda Edge.

This edition published 2010
Reprinted 2013, 2014

ISBN: 978 1 906610 11 1
E-book ISBN: 978 1 908284 97 6

British Library Cataloguing-in-Publication
Data – A catalogue record for this book is
available from the British Library.

Design, typesetting and graphics by Efex Ltd.
Printed in UK.

Contents

Foreword

Research consistently demonstrates how important teaching and learning and classroom processes are in ensuring school effectiveness. When all other things are taken into account (leadership, theories, policies etc), the fact is that it all comes down to what you do every day in the classroom. In particular, teacher effectiveness is about:

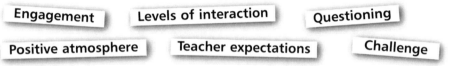

Engagement   Levels of interaction   Questioning

Positive atmosphere   Teacher expectations   Challenge

At the heart of all of these areas is the **ability to communicate effectively.** How you do that, not just on a day-to-day basis but minute-by-minute and second-by-second, is fundamental to what your pupils will learn and remember, and to how they behave.

In this Pocketbook you will find a broad spectrum of tips, tools and techniques to enhance your communication skills. These have been drawn from a wide range of areas including psychology, language models from hypnosis (particularly how to create suggestions more effectively), NLP (neuro-linguistic programming) and neuroscience. Each section aims to give you not just the 'what' but 'how you can do it' in a quick and easily understandable way.

Introduction

What effective teachers do

If there is a recipe for teacher effectiveness, its main ingredients are these:

1. Quality subject knowledge.
2. Understanding of best practice in teaching the subject areas that you cover.
3. A passion for working with children and learners.
4. Excellent communication skills.

This Pocketbook is about the fourth ingredient. It contains tips and strategies to help you develop your use of words and body language. There are also sections to help you communicate more effectively in relation to learning and memory and to support classroom management in general.

The next three pages introduce some **general ideas and theories** about communication. It is important to have these in mind before we explore the **four key areas** of effective communication on page 10 and then go on in the rest of the book to look at **specific strategies** you can use as a teacher.

Communication loops

It's all too easy to slip into a style of communication in which you are really only communicating with yourself. Communication is a two-way process. There is a constant feedback loop between the people involved. For this reason, effective communicators recognise that *the meaning of their communication is the response they get.*

To be an effective communicator you need to **engage actively** in the communication process:

- Pay attention to the way your communication is received (notice details: facial expressions, changes in skin tone, what changes in people's eyes, voice tone, etc)

- Put yourself in the other person's shoes

- Be prepared to adapt the way you say things and pay attention to your body language when you communicate. If what you're doing doesn't get you what you want, do something different!

Interpersonal, intrapersonal

Good teachers need both **interpersonal skills** (the ability to work with others) and **intrapersonal capacity** (the ability to manage yourself and your emotions).

Recent neuroscience shows that brains develop in response to the environment they experience (a process known as plasticity). Your communication skills are as much part of the environment that your learners experience as are your classroom and the resources you use.

- You need to focus on *the way* in which you communicate as well as *what* you communicate

- The emotional climate that you maintain in your classroom affects your learners just as much as the quality of your lesson planning

Automatic vs conscious

Recent cognitive neuroscience and psychology have consistently shown that much of what we do is carried out without conscious attention and without awareness. Think about it. Do you remember turning the last page? When did you decide to do that and how did you decide? The process of doing familiar things quickly and without consciousness is known as **automaticity.** Consciousness happens too late in the process to be the controlling factor.

Developing **conscious awareness and attention** is essential for effective communication because it gives you the ability to manage better what you do and say. In the classroom:

- Ensure clarity and focus of attention
- Create variety and opportunities for as much conscious thinking as possible
- Teach explicitly the routines and processes that you want to see in the classroom
- Use strategies to enhance conscious awareness and improve memory when learning (There are several of these later in the book.)

Four keys to improving your communication skills

Excellent and effective communication is characterised by four elements:

1 **Knowing** what you want.

2 **Noticing** whether you are getting what you want (in particular paying attention to the details of what is going on around you).

3 Having the **flexibility** to change, and a toolkit of alternative behaviours and attitudes that you can draw upon.

4 Doing something about it – **taking action**.

Let's look more closely at these.

Step 1 – do you know what you want?

The first key to success is knowing exactly what you want from a moment of communication. Be clear about the specific behaviours you expect as well as the learning outcomes you are seeking. This will help you to align everything you communicate to achieving this.

For big goals you will want to spend time visualising and thinking through the stages. With practice you can quickly check in and create an image of what you want, what it will be like and whether it is right for you:

- What will you **see** when it happens?
- What will you **hear** when it happens (external sounds and your internal dialogue)?
- What will you **feel** (physically and emotionally)?
- Ask yourself if this behaviour and action is in line with your values

So, if your goal is to introduce a new activity, create a clear picture in your mind of what it will look like when you are doing it (as if you were watching a movie). Become aware of your voice and specific words as well as your internal dialogue (self-talk). Notice what you feel emotionally and physically (how will you stand when successful?). Finally, identify why this is important to you. The more detail you add the better. Make changes so each element aligns with success.

Step 2 – are you noticing what is happening?

Once you begin to notice the details of communication that are going on around you in the classroom (more on this later), you will be in a much better position to know whether your outcome is going to happen or whether you might need to adapt and do something else. Be aware of:

- Body posture (eg leaning forward or backward)
- Facial expressions (eg muscle tension and changes in facial colouring)
- Voice tone (eg pitch, speed of voice and the tone quality used)
- Breathing (eg shallow or deep, quick or slow)
- The type of words your students use (eg notice their preferences for visual, auditory or kinaesthetic words; or words and phrases that give away psychological preferences (see page 111). Connect with your pupils by using similar language forms

Step 3 – are you flexible enough to change?

Have you ever taught a lesson you didn't think was very good yet someone else who observed it thought it was great? We all experience the world through our senses. This is then combined with our experience and what we are paying attention to at the time to create a representation or map. However, the map is not reality – there is a real world out there. So what you think you need to do to communicate effectively may not be the best option.

- Remember, process is not outcome and there are lots of different ways to crack an egg
- Change how you go about communicating what you want if necessary. Influencing differently does not equal failure to achieve your goal
- If what you are doing isn't getting you your outcome, you will need to do something different – this is as true for difficult classes as it is for difficult colleagues

For instance, sometimes lessons don't go well because we have taught them from a purely 'teacher' perspective (our personal map) without really thinking about the perspectives of all the learners and the wider context for the lesson (the reality). A top tip is to sit in the pupils' seats and imagine the lesson from their point of view before they come in. Move around the classroom and think about the lesson from different learner perspectives.

Step 4 – are you taking action?

The final key to successful communication is to really do something. Take action. Too often in teaching we start by changing what we think rather than what we do.

Remember, the map is not reality – your image of the world in your mind is an interpretation of reality, not reality itself. You can spend a lifetime thinking about something but unless you do something about it nothing will change or happen.

- If a particular way of teaching a topic doesn't work, change it – create a new, very different activity
- If a way of explaining something doesn't seem to be working when you look at the details of response from your pupils, adapt it – use different words

Using Words to Influence

Influential language in the classroom

Improving your communication skills in the classroom is about putting in place small changes that make a big difference rather than big changes that make a small one. Frequently, the only difference between two teachers delivering the same lesson in the same way, one of which gets positive compliance and successful learning and one which doesn't, is the way they use language to explain things, introduce topics and encourage learning and behaviour.

Many of the influential language patterns introduced in this section are used successfully in hypnosis and therapy. Adopting them will help you to:

- Start lessons more effectively, ensuring that what you say is aligned with the way you want things to be done
- Increase the likelihood of your behavioural instructions being carried out
- Be more motivating in the way that you talk about learning
- Ensure that you say what you mean and avoid suggesting the opposite, or leaving the possibility for behaviours and actions that you would rather not have
- Spot students' use of negative language and redirect (or reframe) their thinking

Hidden meanings – presuppositions

Have you ever asked a pupil to do something and then found that they did something different? This can happen even if you think that you have been really clear about what you wanted. Every time we say something we communicate on two levels. There is a surface meaning and also a hidden meaning (or presupposition). It is the hidden meanings that children frequently respond to:

- If I say: *'**When** you have learnt this you **will** be able to carry out your own project'*, then I am suggesting success

- Notice how different the effect of the following could be: *'**If** you are able to do this then you **might** be able to do your own project'*

The use of 'when' and 'will' in the first example sets a positive frame of thinking, whereas the language in the second example suggests a possible negative outcome as well as the possibility of success, leaving the learner with a choice of mindset.

Check that what you are saying not only does the job on the surface, but also that the hidden meaning reinforces your message. You can use suggestion and hidden meaning to support motivation, behaviour and learning.

Double binds

One type of hidden meaning, the **double bind,** uses the offer of choice to influence behaviour and response. People like to be able to choose and children and teenagers are no different. With double binds, however, either choice results in the outcome you want:

- *'Sara, would you like to start by drawing the map or do the questions first?'*

- *'You can work and discuss this in a pair or as a whole table.'*

- *'Reading the example, you might find yourself thinking about what you already know or you may find yourself making new connections.'*

- *'Only do as much revision as you want to in order to get better.'*

Think of double binds as a way of giving choice about 'how' to do something that is not an option.

Don't think of a pink flamingo

What happens when you try not to think of something? For instance, don't think of a pink flamingo... ... No matter how hard you try, you cannot not think of it!

In the classroom it's easy to start talking about what we don't want rather than what we do. Because working memory and conscious awareness is limited and only holds five to nine pieces of information (seven plus or minus two) at any time, it is better to make good use of the limited space in your learners' conscious awareness by telling them what you *do* want rather than what you don't.

Don't think about your rules!

Take a moment to think about some typical classroom rules. How could you reframe the language in the left hand column to point to the behaviours that the teacher might want to see rather than mentioning the ones that they don't?

Rule	How could what is wanted be said more effectively?
Don't run	Walk in the corridors
Don't talk loudly in this activity	
Don't be rude	
Don't fight	

Rather than talk about what you don't want, have a constant schedule of positive reinforcement in which you mention frequently and clearly what you do want.

Take a moment to reflect on your own practice. What will you change?

Using negatives to get what you want

On the other hand, you can use the effect of 'don't' and other negatives deliberately to make subtle suggestions. For example:

'I **don't** know whether you will find this interesting.'

'I'm **not** sure when you will realise how important this is.'

Constructions like these arouse curiosity. They tempt with a subtle challenge and the promise of something intriguing.

Yes tags

Another influential language pattern is the **yes tag.** Disagreeing involves slightly more mental effort than agreeing. Yes tags, or tag questions, make use of this fact by adding a negative question at the end of something that has been suggested in order to increase compliance and the likelihood of agreement.

Examples of yes tags:

- *'You can, **can't you?**'*
- *'That's right, **isn't it?**'*
- *'And when you have got to the end you will know what this means, **won't you?**'*
- *'You will tell me when this happens again, **won't you?**'*
- *'Now that you have finished the questions sheet, you could begin to make some revision notes, **couldn't you?**'*

Now you know about these, you can make use of them yourself, can't you? Nodding while you say a yes tag increases its effectiveness.

Yes sets

It has long been known in psychology that if you first get someone to agree to something small it is easier then to ask for something else. The effectiveness of this increases if you have *a series* of 'small asks' first. In the classroom you can make use of this tendency by using a yes set language pattern. **Yes sets** are frequently used in hypnosis and often feature in the speeches of charismatic leaders.

First say three things that are completely true (things that internally your pupils' minds will automatically say yes to), then make your suggestion:

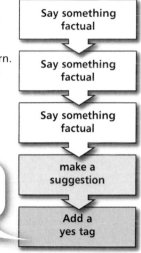

'It is 3.00 pm, we have done the questions and we have looked at the map. Now would be a good time to do some quiet mind mapping for revision, wouldn't it?'

(Notice the **yes tag** at the end of the sentence.
It is quite hard to say no to in this sort of context.)

Say something factual

Say something factual

Say something factual

make a suggestion

Add a yes tag

Yes, yes, yes

Yes sets are a great way to frame an instruction and to communicate what you want more effectively. Two more examples:

- *'As you sit there, listening to me, thinking about how Churchill led Britain in the Second World War, you could begin to think about the way in which you are going to prepare to revise this work. So turn to the person next to you and discuss...'*

- *'We have done some maths, finished off our art work and done a little reading today, so now would be a good time to put our books away and tidy everything up, wouldn't it?'*

You have read about hidden meanings, learnt about yes sets, know about yes tags, now would be a good time to learn some more patterns, wouldn't it?

Softly, softly

Soft language patterns are words and phrases that can be used before suggestions or commands to reduce the chance of resistance or disagreement. Using them in the classroom, particularly where you have challenging students, reduces the possibility of resistance. Effective examples include: *'perhaps you can'*, *'I wonder whether'*, *'maybe you could'*, *'you may'*, *'I'm curious to know'*.

Instead of just telling the students to do something, add some soft patterns:

- *'**I'm curious** to know how many questions you can think of about this topic.'*
- *'**Maybe** you could start more quietly this time, Erica?'*
- *'**You may** begin to wonder what are we going to do when fossil fuels run out.'*
- *'**Perhaps** one of you could tell me how electricity can be made from fossil fuels?'*

Embedding instructions

It can be more effective to embed an instruction within a sentence than to state it directly. This is a useful technique when you want to tell students how you'd like them to do something but don't want to interrupt talking about the learning. Embedding instructions allows you to do both at the same time. Some examples:

- *'Things that may come into your mind as you **read the questions quietly from now on** could include thoughts about what beliefs Henry VIII had'*
- *'As you are about to **complete the exercises on your own** you can begin to **see the importance of completing all the work**'*
- *'Now that you have finished Section A **you will find the next part easy**'*
- *'The index in your text book can be helpful **when you want to know more about this**'*

We know from hypnosis (where it is known as 'the hypnotic voice') that slightly lowering your voice tone and volume as you say the embedded instruction can add to its effectiveness.

Walking in other people's footsteps

To persuade people or groups to do something, you need to understand where they are coming from. The first step is to notice their perspective and explain and talk about things from that point of view – or in the same way that they do. This is sometimes called **pacing**. After you have paced enough to build a connection with the other person you can then **lead** them by making suggestions. Try the following tips for effective pacing and leading:

- Imagine the world through the eyes of the class you are teaching (you might even give them an activity to do where they can talk about their values and what they want)

- When pacing and leading make sure you pace enough. The proportions 2:1 (**pace – pace – lead**) or 3:1 (**pace – pace – pace – lead**) work best

- You can pace by matching such things as: the type of sensory language a person prefers; body language; voice tone; the way they like to do things, eg common interests and psychological preferences (see page 111); or just by listening more first

Connect for influence

Some words are very useful when seeking to influence because they imply a connection between things that are not really connected. This kind of **linkage language** works particularly well when you connect something the pupil is experiencing by pacing and leading as described on the previous page.

- *'**As** you read this section you could begin to think of all the ways this could be useful'*
- *'**Because** you have understood the basics you will now find this next section really easy'*
- *'**And** you can start this quietly just as you did with the first activity'*
- *'**When** you have completed the diagram you will find that the questions make more sense'*
- *'**While** you sit there listening to these instructions you can begin to think of questions that you might want to ask'*

Useful linkage language
- As
- Because
- And
- When
- While

Someone said

> *I met a person the other day in a coffee shop who told me about a friend who had discovered a really effective method of influencing people in a way that they were unaware of.*

Take a moment to have a look at the language pattern in the sentence above. In hypnosis (an area which has a deep understanding of how to influence with language) this is called ***extended quotes.*** Embedding in the sentence what you want to say as if another person has said it is a highly effective way of influencing. The same process is used in advertising (eg getting a 'housewife' to recommend a washing powder rather than the company's CEO!). In the classroom, to support learning you might say:

- *'Several of the sixth form students were telling how they had **overcome the same problems** in motivating themselves to revise by creating a revision diary'*

- *'When I was at school I had a friend who said that you could **be really good at this type of problem with the following solution**'*

Notice also how in the example at the top of the page there was some added visual detail (the coffee shop), another great way of increasing influence.

It's just a story...or is it?

Milton Erickson, the hypnotherapist who was studied by Richard Bandler and John Grinder (the co-founders of NLP), used storytelling as a key way of influencing during hypnosis. As well as influencing NLP, Erickson's work also created a whole school of hypnotherapy. Stories are not just influential in therapy. Our brains are hardwired to listen for and to create meaning out of stories and there is evidence that they may provide the opportunity for mental rehearsal ahead of learning.

- In the classroom start the learning off with a story or metaphor that sums up or illustrates the key things that the pupils are going to learn (for example, you might tell a story about a ship and its captain before going on to discuss an historical situation that has the same basic plot)

- When working with a pupil who is stuck and can't grasp a concept, use a metaphor to help 'un-stick' their thinking (for example, you might use the metaphor of a seesaw or set of scales to help them understand the mathematical concept of equation – where expressions either side of the equals sign need to amount to the same thing)

Time for a change

Language that places things in a time frame (past/present/future) is loaded with presuppositions. Notice the differences in the following and in what they presuppose for learning:

- *'You may have found this sort of thing difficult in the **past**'*
- *'You may **now** find this difficult'*
- *'You may find this difficult in the **future**'*

The first pattern presupposes that the difficulty is now behind the learner rather than in the lesson now or something yet to be dealt with. By contrast, the other two patterns are more likely to have a negative effect on motivation and self-belief because the difficulty is now suggested to be present or still a problem yet to be faced.

Once you have placed a problem in the past (linguistically) you can also then reframe it by presupposing current success and even success in the future. For example:

- *'You may have found this sort of thing difficult in the past but in this lesson **you will learn a strategy that will make it easy today and in the future**'*

Language to reinforce learning

Carol Dweck's research* suggests that the mindset learners develop about where ability comes from is critical to success. Having a 'growth' mindset in which success and intelligence are seen as being the result of hard work and learning is better than seeing intelligence as fixed. Praising and rewarding to encourage a growth mindset is therefore very important. Avoid simplistic praise which implies that intelligence is fixed and predetermined (eg *'You are very clever'*). Instead, concentrate on areas such as:

- Focus
- Learning strategies
- Persistence in overcoming challenges
- Willingness to take on new, more difficult areas of learning

Condition your students to behave and learn effectively through the use of a continuous process of praise and reward. Praise them frequently and be very specific about the things you like. Draw up a list of the details of what you'd like to see from a class, and every time you see someone doing one of these things praise them and point it out (see pages 105-106). Make sure your language presupposes or suggests praise and positive outcomes.

Mindset: The New Psychology of Success by Carol Dweck. Random House, 2006

Words to use with care

As we've seen, the key to influencing with words is to be aware of the hidden meanings in your language. In some cases individual words can contain powerful presuppositions on their own. Think about these words:

If – presupposes option, choice and possibility. Fine if that is what you want to say, but not ideal otherwise. In the classroom, saying *'if you do that again...'* suggests a repetition of the behaviour!

Try – presupposes the possibility that something might not work. Avoid when suggesting things you want to happen.

But – presupposes rejection of what has just been said. Watch how you use it. If you disagree with someone and use the word *'but'* straight after they have expressed their opinion, you may get 'push-back' simply because of your choice of word. Prefacing your alternative argument or viewpoint with the word *'and'* is less threatening.

Top tips for improving your language skills

As with any new field of learning, it's good to take your learning about influential language one step at a time. As mentioned earlier, it's an area where small changes can make a big difference without you having to alter any of the content of your lessons or the way you teach it.

How to get started:

1. Pick one or two of the language patterns you feel most motivated to have a go at using. Gradually build these into your language repertoire in the classroom. Yes Sets (page 23) are a great place to start.

2. Script a few openings to lessons and parts of lessons, deciding in advance what you want to suggest and presuppose.

3. Teach some patterns to others. Teaching others will give you much better retention.

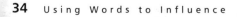

Body Language and Non-Verbal Communication

Everything I do, I do it to you!

Two fundamental ideas to bear in mind for effective classroom communication are:

1. You are always communicating, whatever you do

2. The meaning of your communication is the response you get

Even if you stand still and say nothing, you will be communicating something, depending on the context.

Take control of all levels of your communication by becoming fully aware of your body language while you are talking. In particular, notice the responses that you get from learners and recognise that these responses are the result of what you have done and that you may need to do something different if your communication is not working.

The importance of non-verbal communication

It is hard to overstate the importance of non-verbal communication. Albert Mehrabian, Emeritus Professor of Psychology at UCLA, spent many years studying communication. He found that when a listener is unsure about what is being said or when there is any confusion or 'incongruence' in the communication, they will default to body language or voice tone ahead of the actual words used in the following proportions: **55% body language, 38% voice tone and only 7% words.**

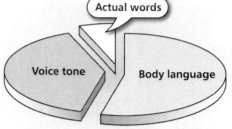

The importance of body language in the classroom was reinforced in an amazing study by Nalini Ambady and Robert Rosenthal who were able to demonstrate that students can predict a teacher's effectiveness when viewing only very short (less than 10 second) video clips of a teacher with the sound turned off!

Styles of physical communication

Some types of body language seem to send out universal signals. Virginia Satir, the family therapist, used a number of these in her practice and this knowledge has been incorporated into NLP and some other forms of therapy. The Satir Categories are:

- Blamer
- Placater
- Leveller
- Computer
- Distracter

It must be you!

The **Blaming posture** involves pointing at the other person. It is a position that says *'it's all down to you'* and implies fault and hierarchy. Although many writers on communication advocate building rapport by matching the other person's body language, this is the one pattern to avoid imitating. Two 'Blamers' often get into an argument, whether they intended to or not.

- Avoid using in the classroom. People with a Blamer preference may see this as a challenge

- To influence a person who is using the Blamer posture, adopt the Placater pattern (palms up) but state what you want assertively and end your statement with the Leveller pattern (palms down). By using Placater you will have given the Blamer what they want, submission, but without actually giving in

I give in

In the **Placating posture** your palms face upwards. Don't use Placater too much as it's a submissive posture and not at all assertive. (Teachers who over use Placater often get walked over by difficult classes).

- Use Placater in the classroom when telling people things that you want to appear as a gift (eg feedback and complicated information)

- If you have used Placater to make a difficult point to someone, end the sentence with Leveller (the next, more assertive pattern)

You know it's true

The **Leveller posture** looks grounded and assertive. Stand in a centred way with your palms down and hand/s slightly in front of you.

- A great posture to use when you want to be assertive or explain rules

- Also useful when giving information. What you say will come across as being true and on the level

- This position is very effective when you want to hold people's attention (you can do this with just one hand)

As with all these postures, you only need to give a hint of it for it to be effective. It's not necessary to adopt a stylised or awkward pose.

Let me think about that

When we see someone thinking, we are often prompted to become more thoughtful ourselves. The **Computing posture** does just that. Stand with one hand or fist under your chin and with that arm's elbow resting on your other arm – which is held across the body. Use Computer to:

- Indicate interest and curiosity after asking a question

- When you want to promote thinking in a meeting

Adopting this posture can also affect your own internal state, allowing you to feel more detached.

I'm not really here

The least assertive of all postures and one to avoid in class most of the time is called **Distracter**. When people are 'distracting' they move between different postures looking inconsistent. The message given out is please don't take notice of me.

- Distracting often occurs with new teachers when they start to feel nervous. In these situations train yourself to adopt Leveller more often and you will come across as more assertive and in control

- The Distracter approach can work quite well if you are telling jokes. It is commonly used by stand up comics and can have its place in the classroom

Step by step

Sequencing is a further category of body language and is useful when you want people to notice that you are teaching about stages in a process or steps in a journey. As you speak, allow your hand to move side on in steps horizontally across your body. You can also do the same gesture moving away from you and towards the other person.

In the classroom:

* Use this gesture when explaining the steps in a learning process or

* Use it when you want your students to understand that what you are talking about is sequential

Another way to use the gesture is to start with your hand out in front and move it back towards you. This says *'let's back track from where we currently are'*. Use it to reinforce on occasions when you say things like *'I think we need to go back a few steps here and think again'*.

The block and remove gesture

As you tune into body language you will start to notice other effective gestures, postures and approaches. Model these by building them into you own practice. Remember to reflect on and test their impact and effect.

One powerful gesture is the 'block and remove gesture'. It is useful when you want to put someone on hold or show that an idea is unrelated without saying so directly in a whole class context.

- Look at the pupil you are talking to and move your hand down and between you as you say what it is that you wish to say that is different
- Then push your palm outwards and away from you as if pushing the pupil away and look at someone else to finish the sentence. If you make eye contact with the next pupil and ask them a question then the discussion will usually move on

Note that this is a strong gesture but can be very effective in the right context.

How we understand each other

Simply observing another person moving activates similar areas in your brain to those that would be activated if you were to move in that same way. In other words, when you see another person doing something, your brain does the same thing too. **Mirror neuron** activity is believed to be important in allowing for the understanding of meaning and may be the key to social intelligence and social literacy. (Autistic children have been shown to have dysfunctional mirror neuron networks.)

In the classroom:

- Build rapport by doing whole group activities and actions
- Support learning by using physical **modelling** of skills where the pupils observe you or others doing something in the most effective way
- Notice the imitation that goes on by the pupils in the groups you teach to help you understand how they are responding to you and each other
- Use social interaction games to support emotional and group development

Show you are listening

Connecting with people is just as important as the language you use when you communicate. This is as true when communicating with children and young people as it is with adults. To show that you are listening:

- Choose to put yourself in a frame of mind and adopt an attitude where you are genuinely interested and not just pretending to listen
- Maintain eye contact
- Show interest by asking questions and clarifying what is meant in relation to the words that are used by others
- Pay attention to body language and check in on your own to make sure that your non-verbal communication is aligned with what you want to say. For instance, are you pointing (even slightly) at the other person when your intention is to be supportive?

Bridge of light

Being in rapport with someone else is as much about your **intention to connect** with another person, as it is about any actions you take, or things you might do or say. The 'bridge of light' is a really quick and effective visualisation for helping you to align your intentions with your actions. Here's how to do it:

- First decide to have a positive relationship with the person you are in contact with – make this your intention

- Make eye contact and as you do this imagine a bridge of light connecting and growing between you

- As any feelings develop inside, just allow yourself to go with the flow and smile when you feel ready to (often the person will smile back as they connect)

- Pay attention to the signals that you get back from the other person and maintain your positive intention to connect

As with many such approaches having a genuine positive intention is key.

Noticing the detail

At the start of this book we identified one of the keys to effective communication as knowing whether you're getting what you want. Darwin was the first person to note that animals give off a wide range of **display signals** – some universal; others unique. People are no different. A typical human display signal, for instance, is blushing. However, because we are able to experience a very wide range of emotions and there is so much individual variation in experience, the signals we give off are often unique to us. Therefore, you need to 'calibrate' what you see to each individual.

To do this, take time to notice the detail of your students' facial expressions and body language. Take mental snapshots of individuals' facial expressions that you are certain are associated with particular feelings. When those expressions are subsequently used, unaccompanied by verbal clues or indicators, you can often pick up what is being felt but not said. Your stored snapshots will help you to read internal states and emotions.

Many display signals are automatic and happen without awareness, eg facial muscle tone, skin colour changes, eye movements, breathing rate, blink rate, voice tone and eye pupil dilation.

Sense and sense-ability

You can develop your **sensory acuity** by doing some simple activities with others, one-to-one or in groups. Use the idea below with a group of colleagues, perhaps as part of an INSET session.

1. Sit opposite another person and take a visual snapshot of what they look like – close your eyes, get them to make a slight movement then open your eyes again. See how good you can get at picking up smaller and smaller movements.

2. Next get the person to think of two different things (something they really dislike and something they really like).

3. Take a mental snapshot of each and see if you can tell which of the two emotions (dislike/like) the person you are working with is thinking of. If you are doing the guessing, close your eyes while the person adjusts their thoughts. Take it in turns and work with different people to learn to spot more and more things.

4. Finally, working together as a group, write down all the small details that allowed you to tell the difference between the two emotions. Think about what you could do with this knowledge.

This activity also works well with children and teenagers in the context of developing emotional awareness of others and relationship awareness.

Small things matter with you too

Asking colleagues or pupils for feedback when you are working with them is a good way to develop your skills further. Ask questions like: *'How are you feeling about this?'* You can confirm whether your own interpretation is correct with 'checking-in' questions like: *'I noticed that you raised your shoulders when I said that; are you still feeling OK about what we are talking about?'*

It is also important to begin learning to manage your own **micro communication.** Paying attention to the key body language categories discussed earlier is one way to do this but you could also decide to focus on a category of detail each day, eg:

- Concentrate on your facial muscles and how they feel when you are in different emotional states

- Monitor your breathing and notice what happens to it in different situations

- Ask a colleague to give you feedback on your body language and how they think you come across. (Remember that feedback is just information and adopt the mindset: there's no failure, there's only feedback.)

Spaces and places

We talked earlier about using praise to condition the pupils in your class to respond in the way you want. Another influential technique is to use **where you stand** to communicate the type of activity or action that is about to happen. You will need to be consistent and also ensure that you use appropriate body language and have the right mental attitude and emotional state when you stand in particular spots. Here's how:

- Have a place in the classroom from where you always ask questions. Use the Computer body language posture (page 42) to convey curiosity and thinking

- Have an assertive, calm space where you adopt the attitude and tone of voice you need to reinforce rules convincingly or to explain expectations. Use the Leveller posture for this (page 41)

- You can also designate spaces for giving information, ending activities and for dealing with behaviour

Signals for attention

One of the things that inexperienced teachers in particular find difficult is to get the attention of a class or to get them to quieten down. There are usually two reasons for this. First, the teacher does not have a clear **signal for attention** that they have explained to the class. Second, even if they have decided on such a signal they are not using it consistently and reinforcing it by reminding the students of its purpose if it doesn't work one time. It is also critical to praise pupils for responding to the signal, especially when establishing it.

Good signals for attention are unusual and will be noticed even when the students are absorbed in their work, eg:

- Tapping a coin twice on the desk
- Ringing a Buddhist-type chime or bell
- Using particular music to indicate the end of an activity or to signal 'tidy up time'

Using your voice effectively

Voice tone communicates a lot of information, particularly when you are dealing with behaviour issues. For instance, cultivating the quiet 'telling off' voice can be really effective. Take some time to reflect on your voice tone and the effect it has. Pay attention to:

- How high or low your voice sounds. Often voice pitch communicates feelings and emotions

- The speed at which you talk. How quickly you talk affects others, so notice the reaction to your current speed and adjust it until you get the right reaction

- The quality of your tone of voice. It's easy to sound harsh when you don't mean to

- Volume. It's easy to 'over project' or 'under project' your voice. Pay attention to this and think about the effect on others in the classroom and the staff room. A loud, 'shouty' voice can be very distracting for learners

Exercises to develop vocal control

New teachers in particular often have problems with their voice and can sometimes lose it in the first term. This is because they have not learnt to use their **diaphragm** like trained singers and actors. Below are two simple exercises to help you work on this:

- Your diaphragm is just below your ribs. Tie a scarf around this area and push your muscles hard against it. Hold for 30 seconds and let go. Repeat 10 times each day for a few weeks and when you speak in the classroom focus your attention on using your diaphragm this way – as if you still had the scarf on

- When out for a walk, take a breath from your diaphragm and as you walk purse your lips, as if giving a kiss, and slowly push the air out from your diaphragm. Count the number of steps you can do and repeat, increasing the number each time

Mark it out

Emphasising certain words or parts of sentences with a particular voice tone can be very useful when you are seeking to influence indirectly in the classroom. For example, when making an embedded suggestion like those on page 26 and the one below you might use a different voice tone – more gentle, lower, reassuring but assertive.

*'When you have learnt this **you will be able to carry out your own project**.'*

Experiment and see what works for you. Eventually you may find a specific tone and pace that works when you use it consistently and for this purpose alone.

Introduction

 Using Words to Influence

 Body Language and Non-Verbal Communication

 Feelings, Emotional Climate and Learning ◀

 Explaining, Organising and Introducing Learning

 Effective Questioning

 People, Mind and Brain Processes

 Reflective Summary

Feelings, Emotional Climate and Learning

Creating the right emotional climate

It is becoming increasingly recognised that learning is fundamentally an emotionally-based activity. Studies of neurological function during learning show that effective brain functioning is dependent on there being a positive emotional environment. However, the need to create the right emotional climate in schools is frequently put to one side or ignored.

Stress, anxiety, tension and anger can all have a negative effect on learning and this is true for the adults in a school as well as the children. This chapter contains information and ideas to help you communicate and create the right emotional climate for learning. There are also techniques for managing your own emotions and feelings.

Emotional climate and neuroscience

Whereas logic and reason used to be seen as separate from feelings and emotions, recent science – particularly the work of Antonio Damasio – suggests that feelings are involved in *all* consciousness and that you cannot separate emotion, feeling and bodily sensation from the process of thinking. It has also been shown that emotions and memory are fundamentally connected. Emotion and mood affect memory and memories frequently involve emotion. In turn, emotional events are better remembered that non-emotional events – something that is particularly true of negative emotions.

- Learners need emotional competence to be effective learners which is why it is so important to include emotional and social literacy components within your practice

- It is particularly important for young people to learn to control impulsive behaviour and manage their emotional reactions to situations

- Stress, anxiety and fear can all have an effect on the students in your classroom by reducing their ability to focus their attention and therefore successfully encode memories of the learning

The Feeling of What Happens: Body, Emotion and the Making of Consciousness
by Antonio Damasio, Vintage publications, 2000

The power of context

Context is also a powerful communicator and one that creates a response. The next time you are working with a group of students, right at the start of the lesson say, *'stand up'*. Then ask them why they stood up. They will usually respond, *'because you said so'*. Now ask them if they would have stood up on a bus if a stranger had instructed them to. Of course they wouldn't. This is a great way to start a discussion about context.

As a teacher you can capitalise on the power of context by applying it to your practice:

1. Your classroom is a different context to the classroom context of others; you cannot, therefore, rely on overarching school rules to create behaviour. You need to establish yourself with all of your pupils.
2. Make your students aware of the 'big picture context' of the learning they are doing and how it relates to the wider world, other subjects and the lesson.
3. Share the context of your learning plans and schemes of work (point out how many lessons are left before a test or exam and what will be in each one).
4. Effective learning is about relationships as well as behaviour. Make sure that positive relationships are part of your classroom context.

A bit of brain chemistry

The communication that children receive has an effect on their brain and learning because of the effect of neurotransmitters. These are chemicals that allow signals to pass between one neuron and another. Signals or impulses (which are like brief spikes of electrical energy) travel down the neuron's axon towards the synapse, the gap between neurons. At the end of the presynaptic terminals the release of chemicals is triggered and the effect cascades through the brain.

When you communicate, you have an effect on other people's brain chemistry and their response in turn affects yours. This is why your own emotional management skills and communication skills are so important.

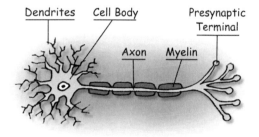

The feelgood factor

Some people argue that the mind, brain and body system extends not just down through our nervous system but also out to others through the activation of parts of the brain associated with social relationships and possibly even social systems (such as mirror neurons). Things to remember:

- Recognise your emotions and become more aware of how you are feeling before and when you are teaching

- Your **emotional state affects your students** because you will be communicating those emotions through voice tone, body language and what you say

- Learn some techniques like anchoring (see opposite) to help you manage your responses and be more emotionally aware

Anchoring

Anchoring is a helpful technique for managing emotions and feeling. Here's how to do it:

- Decide in advance on a feeling or mood you want to have in a situation (for instance, you may be about to face a particularly difficult parent and you know that it will be important to remain calm and assertive)

- Think of a time when you felt like that. Imagine all the details, notice what you see, hear and feel. Let the feelings increase until they are nearly at their height

- Do something unique (touch a knuckle for example) and hold this as the feelings grow

- Let go just as the feeling is about to reach the height of its sensation

- Test your work by re-activating the stimulus

You can use anchoring with classroom spaces (page 52). In the place you stand if you need to reinforce rules, for example – a space you associate with calm assertiveness – anchoring can help you to ensure that your body language, words and internal feelings all align.

Four more anchoring ideas

Other ways to manage emotions with anchoring:

- Have a relaxation anchor for the end of the day so you can let go (eg use anchoring to bring back the feelings of calm and 'me time' that you experienced on a holiday once and associate that feeling with a space on the floor in front of a comfortable chair, so you access those feelings again before you sit down to relax)

- Teach anchoring to pupils with emotional, social and behavioural difficulties by having a time-out space – perhaps a chair in an imaginary blue circle that they associate with calmness and thinking

- Associate different spaces in the classroom with different types of learning activity so that students develop expectations about what will happen next

- Add different emotions to an anchor so that it takes on a group of feelings and emotions, for instance: enthusiastic, motivated and relaxed

Stop and think

We've all said things in the heat of the moment and then regretted it. When we have a strong emotional reaction to something, parts of our brain (particularly the amygdala) can override our reason and higher order thinking skills. In extreme situations this can lead to what Daniel Goleman calls an 'amygdala hijack'.

We know the effect that a sudden outburst has on us but don't necessarily think about its impact on learners. In the classroom, not being in control of feelings and emotions can quickly teach pupils not to take risks in their learning and just to keep their heads down. Top tips for developing a stop and think approach:

- Recognise that you can choose how to react and that your emotions are under *your* control, not the control of others

- Check in regularly on you current emotional state and be aware of what's causing it so that you don't react to something that isn't (eg a previous incident or general stress)

- Develop strategies for managing your emotions and feelings (eg give yourself a time-out before dealing with something, or first praise students who are doing the right thing before quietly talking to the one who is not)

Working with Emotional Intelligence by Daniel Goleman. Bloomsbury, 1999

Humour

If you ask pupils across the age range what makes a good teacher, 'having a sense of humour' will rarely be far down the list. They know that effective teachers use humour to defuse awkward situations and build good relationships in the classroom. Studies of relationships in the work environment suggest that humour is able to kick-start creative thinking and ability. Humour stimulates the brain's reward systems, increasing the levels of the neurotransmitter dopamine. For these same reasons humour is important in the classroom.

- Plan for humour (eg keep a little book in which you write down good stories that your pupils will like)
- Create activities that are fun and engaging
- Encourage humour and ensure that you reward appropriate humour when it arises

When you go to see stand up comedy, knowing you are going to laugh is just as influential as the actual first joke. If you like to tell jokes to classes, help to build that sense of anticipation by having a particular place in the room where you stand to do this.

Emotional contagion

Emotions have been shown to be contagious in organisational contexts. They can spread from one person to another with ease and rapidity.

- Remember that when you deal with children and teenagers – particularly those with social, emotional and behavioural difficulties – the emotions, state and mood you leave them in may well have an effect on the next teacher they come into contact with. Be mindful at the ends of lessons to help set a tone that spreads through the whole school

- In the corridors, as you deal with behaviour, think about where the pupil is going next and avoid aiming for a quick win

- Recognise that the learning and processes you have in your classroom do not have just an isolated effect. They are part of a context and affect others

Use it or lose it

Plasticity is the term for the brain's capacity to change its structure and how it functions. There is a growing consensus that experience, in combination with genes and chance, are what shape the brain, and that education and the way it is delivered are fundamental to neural development. One of the processes in plasticity is **neuron migration**.

New neurons are grown when we need them. They are born deep in the brain and migrate for 3-4 weeks. They travel along long fibres called radial glia. These link the inner and outer structures of the brain. Their journey is mapped for them by chemical signals that help them to navigate, but their journey is only successful if the signals continue.

The way to ensure that those signals continue is to revisit the learning and include frequent **repetition and association**. Repetition and association may, therefore, be important not only for memory and retention, but also for longer-term brain development.

Organise the way you communicate learning over time to ensure appropriate revisiting of learning. Make connections and associations relate to long-term goals.

One-to-one

Increasingly, the importance of **mentoring** and **coaching** to assist learning is being acknowledged. Communicating effectively one-to-one is just as important a key skill for teachers as presenting to a whole class. You can refine your one-to-one communication skills by practising listening and questioning technique (more on effective questioning on pages 83 – 100).

- If you are the sort of person who drifts off into your own thoughts when someone is talking, practise the **repeated word method**. In your own mind repeat to yourself what has just been said to improve your focused attention. Eventually you won't need to

- Adapt your attitude as well as skills. Decide to be interested and adopt a non-judgemental stance

- Notice when people use broad generalisations or delete information, and ask questions for clarity. This shows interest and gets you the information you need

- Check what people mean by certain words

- Exchange more personal information to build and demonstrate trust

Developing your coaching skills

Effective coaching is about helping people (through questioning) to identify the gap between where they currently are and where they want to be so that they can plan next steps and actions. The same process in thinking can be very powerful in the classroom:

1. Help your pupils to be clear about what their goals are and what they want to achieve. Use a questioning style to challenge them to think this through.
2. Use questioning to clarify the current situation and where they are now.
3. Get them to identify next steps that will fill the gap between their current reality and their goal.
4. Have them make a record of what they plan to do.
5. Reward the achievement of small steps to support motivation and attainment.

Developing a coaching style in the classroom is also a great way to bring together many of the skills we have so far covered in this book.

Explaining, Organising and Introducing Learning

The neuroscience of brain connection and learning

It is brain interconnectivity that most enables intelligence.

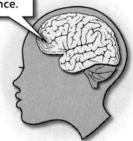

Different parts of the brain do not turn completely on and off in different contexts and neither do they work in isolation. A good way to picture this is to think of an orchestra where all musicians might play at once but at any particular time there is a soloist or group of soloists. **Interconnectivity** is a key part of brain functioning, and creating interconnectivity is critical in learning and teaching.

Consequently, as teachers, we should aim to structure learning in a way that ensures the maximum possible connectivity. For instance, you can cover a range of thinking about a topic in a multi-sensory way with variety and repetition and ensuring that you make explicit associations. (See the following pages on memory and neuroscience).

What to say about memory

We now know quite a lot about the **neuroscience of memory**. Making sure that students understand the key processes is just as important as developing approaches that are in line with them yourself as a teacher. Things to convey to your pupils:

- Memory can be improved with the right strategies

- Attention is important in memory. We often forget things because we didn't encode the information properly in the first place

- Memory is an active process. *Doing things* improves recall

- Memory-aids and compensatory methods help learning (revision cards, other ways of presenting things, summaries, etc)

- If you place importance on the thing that you are learning by doing other things around it, this tells your brain that the central thing is important and you are more likely to remember it. (Probably why mind mapping works well for many people – provided it's done carefully and with a positive mindset)

Attention

It is the process of attention that directs consciousness. Attention works like a sort of highlighter pen, making some parts of our experience stand out while others disappear into the background. The process of attention selects aspects of the environment that are most important at that moment in time and amplifies your brain's response to this. So:

- Have strategies in the classroom that get your students' attention
- Make them explicitly aware of the importance of focusing their attention so that they encode information well
- Ensure you communicate in ways that support attention by scheduling suitable breaks and changes of activity so that attention does not drift
- A good phrase to have in mind is **'the teacher who sets the frame leads the communication and the learning'**. In other words, the way you introduce a topic will affect the way the learning is perceived by your students and will affect what they pay attention to later in the topic. Help your students by making explicit what they should be focusing their attention on

Connecting memory with well-being

Learners are not necessarily aware of the connection between their physical well-being and the brain's ability to remember well. Make sure your students understand just how interconnected the mind, brain and body are. Explain that:

Mind and body are part of a single system. Therefore, **nutrition** – particularly levels of B12 and Omega 3 – affect learning. For example, research by John Stein of Oxford University has shown that fish oils are beneficial to students with dyslexia and ADHD. They help to increase flexibility in the parts of neurons that transmit electrical impulses.

Stress inhibits learning. When we get stressed particular neurochemicals that can close down higher order thinking surge through the brain and make learning more difficult.

Alcohol shrinks the brain. Abstainers from alcohol have been shown to have 1.6 percent greater brain volume than heavy drinkers.

Exercise improves brain functioning and particularly memory. Some research has even shown that aerobic exercise can increase brain volume in older adults.

Memory and recall strategies

Everything you do communicates something. Some simple strategies can do much to improve learning and memory.

- **Repetition** improves retention and recall. Practice does in fact make perfect – and improves synaptic connections
- Get your students to do things using **multi-sensory** domains at once (eg incorporate visual and auditory by reading aloud)
- **Pictures** are better than words for promoting recall. Use highly memorable visual images to support retention
- Do something really memorable at key points in a topic (eg go outside and do a crazy activity)

More ways to improve memory and recall

Other specific strategies include:

- **Time travels.** Improve memory by getting your pupils to remember the context as well as the content. Introduce key topics in interesting ways or places. When revising with the class refer back to these contexts

- **Imaginary spaces.** Teach your students to use techniques like 'The Roman Room' where they associate different spaces in an imaginary location with aspects of the learning. Get them to draw their room and physically walk around it in a large space. Later, by touring the room in their mind's eye they will be able to recall their learning

- **Chunking.** Chunking information makes it easier to remember. For instance, the number 251210 is easier to remember if you notice the association with Christmas Day and chunk it 25-12-10

Five steps to heaven

It's important to have a structure in mind when communicating across a whole lesson. One way to do this is the Five Steps to Heaven model.

Imagine standing on five different steps as you move to each stage in the lesson. You can also do this from different spaces in the classroom adopting different body language where appropriate.

For example, you may want to use more of the Computer posture in the fourth stage as you ask the class lots of connection questions about what happened in the third activity phase. Use more Leveller and Placater in step 2 and make sure you are motivating at the start.

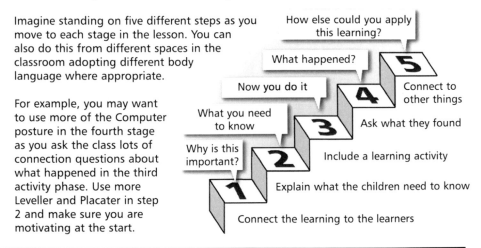

How else could you apply this learning?

What happened?

Now you do it

What you need to know

Why is this important?

5 Connect to other things

4 Ask what they found

3 Include a learning activity

2 Explain what the children need to know

1 Connect the learning to the learners

Motivation

Learning is underpinned by **motivation**. If you are motivated, then you are saying to your brain 'pay more attention to this'. There appear to be two types of motivation:

1. 'Towards' motivation.
2. 'Away from' motivation.

'Towards' motivated learners will be motivated by goals, future outcome and the possibility of rewards.

'Away from' motivated learners will be motivated by moving away from failure or fear.

Cater for both of these types in the language you use when outlining the benefits of learning: talk about **what will happen** when they can do this as well as **what they will have avoided**. When seeking to challenge individual pupils, adapt your approach by aligning what you communicate to their motivational preference.

Break it down

Two key factors in memory are what are known as **primacy** and **recency**. In other words, in any learning episode we are likely to remember the first thing that happened and the last. That's why having a good start to a lesson and an effective summary is critical.

When you explain what will be in the lesson, open your students' minds by chunking what you tell them into clear categories:

- Start by explaining the big picture concept and then break it down
- Summarise what they will learn, breaking down the elements as you would in a well-drawn mind map
- Do this for each element of learning that will take place in the classroom
- Include a learning summary at the start of the lesson as well as at the end

What do you expect?

Expectations or **expectancy** is the big cheese in communication-rich contexts like teaching and learning. For example, it is thought to be a key part of the process in hypnosis (alongside the extent to which a person is hypnotisable and whether or not they want to be hypnotised). In the case of hypnosis, the way the hypnotist 'talks up' hypnosis from the start has an effect on the outcome. Interestingly, education research has shown something similar.

- Make sure that your expectations are clear from the start
- Talk up the possibilities of learning and use language that reinforces the fact that achievement will be possible and even easy
- Build response expectancy by referring to what will be learnt next lesson or even in the next activity as you go along and way before you actually do the things (include the way in which activities will happen)
- Use suggestive language to embed expectancy and expectations as you go along (see pages 15-34)
- Remember to be clear yourself about what it is that you expect so that you can align all your communication (words, body language, emotions, state) to this

Building response potential

There are many ways to build expectancy and response potential in your classroom:

- Use metaphors and storytelling at the start of a lesson. Stories that mirror what is going to be learnt will capture interest and curiosity

- Leave a cliffhanger at the end of a lesson so that students have a desire and expectation of resolution the next time. You can do this with a story or metaphor or through a 'sneak preview' of the next interesting area or question to be explored

- Give problems and problem-focus activities that require new learning to solve them. Your students will desire the knowledge they need to solve them

- When setting out learning, ask pupils what they think they will need to know to solve a problem and build interest and engagement that way

Effective Questioning

Why is questioning important?

We have learnt about language patterns, found out about effective body language and got some new strategies for organising learning, so now would be a good time to zoom in on questions and questioning in the classroom.

Most of what people do happens without conscious awareness – just like when you've driven a car somewhere and don't remember parts of the journey. The same is true in the classroom: students can easily end up on 'unthinking' autopilot. Asking questions frequently – particularly questions that challenge thinking – is an excellent way of creating awareness and prompting as much conscious attention as possible.

> When you ask a good question students are forced to think. When they are thinking there is the potential for learning and behaviour change.

Also, it is easy to fall into the teacher trap of making judgements about how much pupils have learnt by looking just at their behaviour and their written work. Asking challenging questions is a key way of revealing how much has been absorbed and understood.

Six questions, six mindsets

The six classic questions lead our minds in different directions. Take a moment to ask yourself each of these and notice where your mind goes in response to the different words.

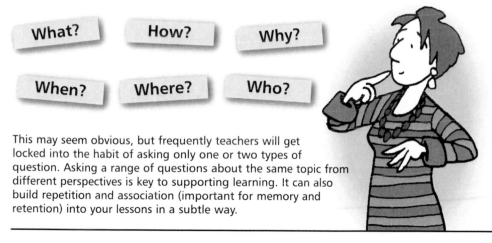

What?　　**How?**　　**Why?**

When?　　**Where?**　　**Who?**

This may seem obvious, but frequently teachers will get locked into the habit of asking only one or two types of question. Asking a range of questions about the same topic from different perspectives is key to supporting learning. It can also build repetition and association (important for memory and retention) into your lessons in a subtle way.

Using the six questions

Take a look at how the six different questions prompt quite different ways of thinking about a single topic:

- *'What is Pythagoras' theorem?'*
- *'How do you calculate it?'*
- *'How could you use it?'*
- *'Why does this formula work?'*
- *'Who would find this useful?'*
- *'Who else?'*
- *'When would they want to use this?'*
- *'When else?'*
- *'Where would this be useful?'*
- *'Where else?'*

Why?

'Why' is one of the most powerful questions to ask when you want people to explore facts and to reason about the causes of things.

However, employ it with caution in the context of behaviour and discipline. When you ask a question, the presupposition (or suggestion) is that you want an answer. This may not be the case with 'why' in a discipline context. For example, *'Why did you do that?'* may elicit a response you don't really want.

The question 'why?' does something interesting to the way people think and sends them back into the past to find information and justification – great for high order thinking about learning but not so good for dealing with behaviour or in a coaching development context. **You can always replace 'why' with a 'what' or 'how' question.**

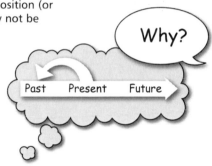

Silence is golden

When you are teaching, how do you know that you have asked a really good question?

If it is a question that has prompted thinking then you will frequently get silence as the class or individual muses, reflects, considers. It's all too tempting to jump in and give the answer. Don't!

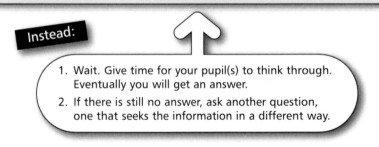

Instead:

1. Wait. Give time for your pupil(s) to think through. Eventually you will get an answer.

2. If there is still no answer, ask another question, one that seeks the information in a different way.

Open the gate or close the door?

Know the effects of different types of question in the classroom.

1. **Closed questions** lead to a yes or no answer. *'Did you do that?'* They get you little information back.

2. **Open questions** prompt thinking. *'What happened?'* They contain the possibility of numerous responses.

3. **Clean questions** show interest and give permission for free *'And that's like what?'* thinking. They make no suggestion about the response you want.

4. **Embedded questions** contain an influential suggestion. *'Can you see the way that this moves?'*

5. **Leading questions** deliberately force a way of thinking or limit responses. *'Is it true that Henry VIII had six wives?'* Not a powerful way of prompting memory and thinking.

On the level?

We have a natural tendency to organise knowledge according to what are known as logical levels of type. Thus a yacht is a type of transport but a sail is part of a yacht. It is easy to end up stuck at one logical level without exploring either the deeper details of an area or the bigger picture implications.

Learners tend to have a preference for specific processing or for bigger picture processes, so you also need to adapt how you explain things when students get stuck. Some will like the detail first, others the big picture

The process of moving between logical levels is known as **chunking**.

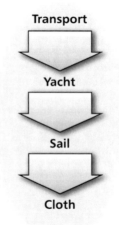

Up a level?

Chunking up involves asking questions that get learners to think on a higher logical level and get a bigger picture view.

Ask questions like:

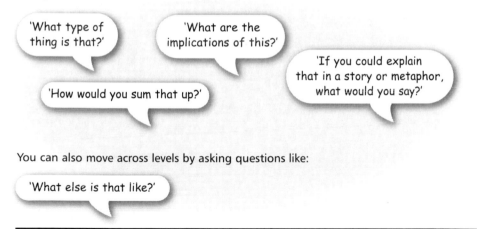

'What type of thing is that?'

'What are the implications of this?'

'If you could explain that in a story or metaphor, what would you say?'

'How would you sum that up?'

You can also move across levels by asking questions like:

'What else is that like?'

Down a level?

Equally, you can discover other meaning and connection at a lower logical level by **chunking down**. In fact it is easy to skip across the surface of meaning and communication without exploring the specifics and details.

Ask questions like:

'What specifically do you mean by X?'

'What are the different components or elements of this?'

'What are the key specific things that allow this to happen?'

'What specifically does that mean?'

See page 97 for more examples of how to ask questions that seek more detail.

Re-frame with the question compass

Our working memory is limited to processing seven plus or minus two chunks of information. Therefore what enters our consciousness is also quite limited. It's a bit like looking through a frame in which things outside the edges are not visible. Outside of the frame, however, may be the information or thinking we need. The same applies to pupils when they get stuck in the classroom. The solution is **re-framing**.

First, notice the type of language a student is using and then ask a question that takes their thinking in an opposite direction. Use the question compass to give yourself some ideas about this – although the number of possible reframes is almost limitless

Re-framing is also a good technique to use when coaching.

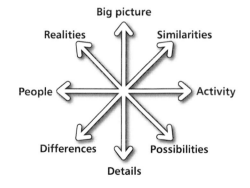

Re-frame to 'un-stick' thinking

The previous page looked at the sort of frames that people operate from and how to take their thinking elsewhere to give them a wider perspective. A person's preferred or current way of thinking can lead them to need one sort of information before they can understand another – such as needing to hear the big picture application for something before being able to grasp the details, or vice versa. (Pages 111-117 explain more about these kinds of psychological preferences.) Here's how it might work in your classroom:

- If a student is struggling to understand detail in a mathematical formula, connect them to the bigger picture. Ask questions about what they think this could be used for, or give examples of what you could do with it

- When working through a relationship, listen to see if the pupil is talking about just facts and actions (having a task focus). Ask them some people questions (eg *'What do you think that Erica would say about this?'*)

- If a pupil is not noticing key information, listen to see if they are just spotting similarities and redirect them to the differences in the data. Ask about this (eg *'So you have noticed all the similar things; which ones are different? What does this tell you?'*)

In all the examples above, the opposite might also be the case. There is no right place to be.

The three basic perceptual positions

It's worth being aware that your students will tend to be thinking from one of three perceptual positions and will tend to have a preference:

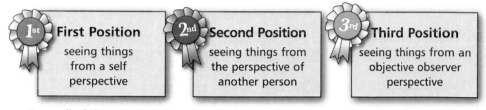

1st First Position
seeing things from a self perspective

2nd Second Position
seeing things from the perspective of another person

3rd Third Position
seeing things from an objective observer perspective

Cover all of these areas in your questioning about topics to ensure that those who are stuck in one way of thinking are challenged to think differently. For example, to focus attention on each of the three positions ask question like:

'What's important to you about that?' *'How do you feel about it?'* (**First Position**)

'What do you think they feel about this?' *'How do they see it?'* (**Second Position**)

'If someone else unconnected to this was looking at the situation what would they say?' *'If you were a fly on the wall, what would this look like?'* (**Third Position**)

Two more perceptual positions

There are two other perceptual positions that are useful when teaching:

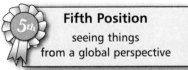

Fourth Position
seeing things from
a process perspective

Fifth Position
seeing things
from a global perspective

Carefully directed questions can move your students to these perceptual positions. To encourage fourth position thinking, you could ask: *'How does this happen?'* *'What's the next best step in this process?'* *'What is going on in this system?'*

Move your students towards a global perspective by asking: *'What's the big picture here?'* *'How would this affect everything else in the world?'* *'If the world could speak what would it say?'*

You can plan lessons using the perceptual positions framework to broaden the way students approach their learning. Explain the concept and then organise the class into groups. Each group explores the topic from a different perspective and then shares what they have learnt.

The question square

The question square is a way of combining the five perceptual positions with the fact that we can also frame our thinking according to whether we are considering the past, present, or future.

For example, you might ask students to answer questions on the topic of global warming from particular areas in the square:

	Self	Other	Observer	Process	The big picture
Past			✓		✓
Present	✓				
Future		✓			

- *'What would an observer from the past say about what we are doing today?'* (Past – Observer)

- *'What would you want to say to people today about this?'* (Present – Self)

- *'What would people from the future want to say to us if they could travel back in time?'* (Future – Other)

- *'If the world had a voice what would it say to someone from the past about where we have got to now?'* (Past – Global)

The question square

You don't need to cover all the areas in the square to have an impact. Simply identify which type of questioning will challenge thinking the most. You can also do this by dividing up spaces in the classroom (past, present, future) and getting pupils to imagine they are travelling in time, as if in Dr Who's TARDIS. Groups stand in the identified areas and discuss the topic from different perspectives. They then share their discussions.

You can teach the question square to your students explicitly so they can use it independently to explore new topics. Or you can simply notice where an individual's thinking is and frame a question from the square to take them somewhere else, moving them towards deeper understanding.

Seven great 'rescue' questions

Quite often when we are questioning in the classroom – particularly in a coaching or facilitating context – it can be hard to come up with the next question but we want to avoid telling and giving answers.

When you are lost for words, have some 'rescue' questions ready so that you can keep asking and challenging thinking. Use questions like:

1. *'Tell me more about that?'*
2. *'What else?'*
3. *'How else?'*
4. *'And that's like what?'*
5. *'If you did know the answer what would it be?'*
6. *'What's the best question that I could ask you now?'*
7. *'How do you know?'*

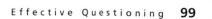

How to redirect questions to avoid telling

Sometimes students will ask you a question in order to get you to give them the answer when what you really want is that they think about things more deeply, or for themselves. This is easy to deal with. Simply redirect them by asking a question back:

'How do I put this section together with the first part that I have built?'

'How do you think that you can put that section with the first part?'

People, Mind and Brain Processes

What's in this section?

It's not just neuroscience, therapy and the language used in hypnosis that can provide useful pointers to classroom communication. There are also many useful pieces of research from the fields of organisational behaviour and psychology that can teach us how to increase classroom effectiveness.

This section contains an assortment of strategies and concepts drawn from various areas. The ideas are broadly grouped as follows:

- First, a look at some ideas from organisational behaviour and organisational psychology that have been applied to an education context, the sort of ideas found in MBA courses

- Then a few more ideas from neuroscience, including a discussion about gifted and talented students and VAK

- Finally, some ways to apply thinking about psychological preference and personality type to your toolkit of influencing and communication skills

Dip in and enjoy!

Understanding group processes

The Group Formation Model comes from the field of organisational behaviour.
As well as being useful in a leadership context, it is helpful in relation to developing classroom communication skills. Bruce Tuckman and Mary Jensen studied group behaviour and noted that there are key stages in the formation of groups:

Forming – during which the group begins to come together and roles are established

Storming – the stage in which there is jockeying for position and power

Norming – roles are established within a hierarchy

Performing – the group is able to become more independent. Empowerment is given and the group as a whole is able to perform to a high standard

These processes and stages apply to leadership and team-working scenarios as well as to classroom contexts.

Tips for group formation

The group formation process can be seen over time and in individual lessons. In your teaching, make sure you get the first two stages (forming and storming) embedded quickly and avoid performing type activities before the pupils are 'normed' to your authority.

Some tips for working with classes at different stages of group development:

- At the **Forming** stage you need to connect with your students and flex your teaching style to ensure that you get to know them and they get to know each other

- At the **Storming** stage the way you deal with behaviour may well define the classroom hierarchy and climate that will follow. Be ready for the first challenge when it comes. Always expect it and deal with it on your terms. Make your values clear

- To ensure **Norming** set clear goals and expectations with clarity and authority

- Once you have your students norming you can empower them at the **Performing** stage. Use more activities with challenging, open-ended tasks

Catch them doing something right

As mentioned earlier, **positive reward** is a key tool to have in your box. It's all too easy to keep mentioning the things you don't want. Instead, use positive reward to communicate what you do want. As you walk around the classroom, continually point out specific things that are happening that are good and that you want to see again, particularly in relation to small details. Using names, praise the pupils engaged in these positive behaviours.

The trick is to thank pupils for doing the right thing rather than focusing on those doing the wrong thing. If a student arrives late, turn to the rest of the class and say: *'Thank you to everyone who was on time today'*. Deal with the latecomer one-to-one when they've sat down and when you're ready. Make your motto for behaviour management:

'Catch them doing something right'

Ways to praise

A good way to get started with a positive reward strategy is to make two lists:

1. List 30 things you want to praise and point out whenever you see them.
2. List as many different phrases as you can think of to deliver praise – you'll be amazed at how many you can come up with. Aim for 40.

What to praise	Ways to praise
Praise small specifics	*'Well done for underlining the title in the way I asked.'*
Thank students for doing the right thing	*'Thank you for being ready to learn so quickly.'*
Show you notice effort	*'I really like the amount of time you have put into this.'*
Use names when praising	*'You have asked a really good question there Andrea, well done.'*
Praise improvements	*'You really have improved your presentation skills, haven't you?'*

VAK – the neuroscience

Time now for a little more neuroscience. We have just seen how praise motivates, so does making sure you have variety in lessons, and this is where some ideas about visual, auditory and kinaesthetic learning styles (VAK) can be useful.

The concept of VAK has been criticised in recent years as the neurosciences show that the brain works through **interconnectivity** and that **all the modalities talk to each other** and therefore cannot be seen as separate. However, recent evidence from the University of Pennsylvania (2009, *The Journal of Neuroscience*) identifies a middle ground in that people who consider themselves visual, as opposed to verbal, tend to convert linguistically presented information into a visual mental representation – a process that takes place nonetheless in an interconnected way.

This does not mean that using VAK approaches will have an effect on attainment. However, thinking about VAK learning styles generally may be helpful in improving communication in the classroom, as we'll discuss in a moment.

VAK and communication

So where does the latest neuroscience place VAK and communication?

It has never been a positive thing to see children wearing badges saying, 'I'm a Visual Learner'. However, VAK can help us as teachers by reminding us of the importance of *all* sensory modality input in learning to support memory. Most memories are associated with events that include **sights, sounds** and **other sensations.** The more intense these sensations are, the stronger the potential for recall.

- If adapting your teaching style to help a pupil understand something by, say, drawing a picture helps, or for other students giving them a list, or a piece of oral work, then do it. (There is also some evidence that matching word preference may influence, build rapport and motivation, but this is not quite the same as learning style)

- Some learning approaches may also be tackled more easily with either a visual, auditory or kinaesthetic emphasis (eg visual stimuli in organic chemistry) and learners clearly benefit from learning strategies that allow flexibility in each of these styles of input

G&T

John Geake's work* suggests that very talented learners have developed more interconnectivity in their brains. You can support and communicate in ways that will motivate such learners with a range of strategies by:

- Including more tasks with high memory demands
- Doing fewer small, repetitive tasks
- Focusing on the skills of analysing and synthesising in the work you set
- Including lessons which go beyond the normal curriculum
- Making sure they already know what they know. (Give them feedback and ensure that assessment is aimed at letting them know which higher order skills they have acquired)
- Making connections between areas of the curriculum clearly and frequently

Of course, *such strategies are useful with all pupils* but it's particularly important to communicate to your high achieving students that you recognise and feel the need to reward their abilities.

The Brain at School: educational neuroscience in the classroom by John Geake. OUP, 2009

Improving performance with visualisation

Another useful concept that you can apply to your classroom practice is **visualisation.**

A number of psychological studies demonstrate that **positive mental rehearsal improves performance,** particularly if the imagined internal landscape contains visual, auditory and kinaesthetic information. Also, all-sensory input has been shown to be more effective in hypnosis for creating change and learning, especially in relation to reducing anxiety. Such techniques are now widely used in sports coaching.

When you have good rapport with a class, you can use eyes-closed visualisation to enhance learning, particularly with tasks and skills:

- Explain the relevance of visualisation to your students
- Use positive language to make connections in the visualisation with the learning
- Include all-sensory information in your visualisation: visual, auditory and kinaesthetic

That's the way I like it

One very good way to connect with your students is to recognise their psychological perspective. People, including children, develop **psychological preferences** in relation to areas such as motivation, working with others, communication style, and information processing.

Just to be clear, I am not talking about learning styles here. Rather, these are things that probably have an effect on motivation that in turn affect whether or not someone is bothered to learn. Nor am I advocating any form of 'setting' or labelling on such a basis. Using psychological preference in the classroom is about adapting your teaching and communication style *in the moment.*

We're going to look at five types of psychological preference (though there are many more) drawn from ideas such as personality type and trait, metaprogrammes and cognitive style:

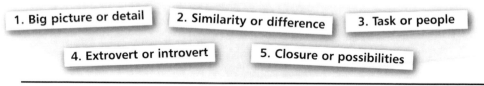

1. Big picture or detail   2. Similarity or difference   3. Task or people

4. Extrovert or introvert   5. Closure or possibilities

1. Big picture or detail?

One key psychological preference that affects learning, because students with different preferences will feel motivated by different ways of presenting information, relates to whether information is presented at a big picture level or at a specific level.

- Those with a big picture preference like to hear metaphor, connections and wider implications in order to make meaning out of information. They need this *before* the detail

- Those with a detail preference will prefer to hear the practical, specific details and then work up from these to the big picture

You will have a preference for one of these yourself. Make sure that your teaching isn't dominated by your own preference. Include both big picture and detail during a lesson and at the start. If one of your students is stuck, notice their preference and give them some information from the other perspective.

2. Similarity or difference?

Another preference that affects our processing and therefore our learning is whether we prefer to notice similarities or difference. Take a look at the this picture and describe it.

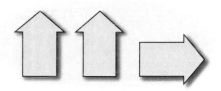

Did you notice the similarities or differences first?

- When planning learning activities be aware of whether the activity emphasises the processes of similarities or differences
- Build both into learning wherever possible
- If an activity has to be in one mode, be prepared to support those in your class who have a different preference to keep them motivated

3. Task or people?

We also have psychological preferences related to whether we tend to focus on tasks or people. This can lead us to prefer certain subjects and even be more motivated to choose one job over another.

- Stretch students with a task preference by discussing issues of importance and values. Help them to see the benefit of making decisions based on feelings as well as facts

- Students with a preference for people over tasks can be encouraged to develop flexibility by being challenged to think about the objective position and to look at things from an observer perspective

Be aware of the focus of the learning in your lesson and ensure that connections are made to both areas of life. If covering a topic in chemistry, for example, go beyond the facts to include the benefits to people and their health. In arts subjects balance creativity with explanations of technique and strategy.

4. Extrovert or introvert?

Extroversion or introversion is one of the big five personality factors and has a particular effect in the classroom. Remember that:

- **Extrovert personality types** will often tend to have a preference for talking things through and working things out aloud in discussions and group work

- **Introvert personality types** will often prefer to think things through before saying something and may need time to come to a conclusion. Just because they are quiet doesn't mean that they aren't doing something. Forcing them to speak straight away can be stressful for them and counterproductive

5. Closure or possibilities?

Another psychological preference that can affect how learners engage with activities, work and revision is related to whether a person prefers to have **closure** or to leave things **open ended**.

- Students with a **closure preference** will respond best to structured activities and will like having clear timescales and objectives. They will be more motivated by working step-by-step over time towards a goal

- **Possibility-preferring learners** will enjoy more open-ended tasks with a range of possible outcomes. They will be more inclined to leave things to the last minute and get a burst of motivation from doing so

Support both preferences by encouraging pupils to develop skills from both perspectives. Ask yourself, which preference you present as a teacher and how you can connect with learners who have a different preference.

The four secrets

There are four steps to effective influencing using people's psychological preference be it within the classroom or more generally:

1. As with all effective communication have a goal in mind. You can't influence someone unless you **know specifically what you want** to achieve

2. **Notice** where someone else is coming from (their map of the world or psychological preference)

3. **Think** about how you would explain this through *their* map of the world

4. **Explain** the idea from where they are coming from

Nature or nurture?

Whether personality type and trait are the result of genetics or environment has been much debated. Today the consensus in psychology is that it's probably a bit of both. Remember:

Children's psychological preferences are still developing and may not be fixed until much later in life, possibly even as late as their twenties.

Flexibility is the key to success in managing your preferences later in life. Help your pupils by not only matching noticeable preferences to create motivation and rapport but also stretching them to work outside their preference – particularly when you see a strong preference already in place.

There is no 'right' psychological preference; it all depends on the context.

Always talk about 'preference', never label a pupil as an 'x' type person – we all have choice and much can be gained by choosing to do something from a different perspective.

The younger a child is the more flexible they will be.

Reflective Summary

Values, school improvement and learning

When it comes to improving your classroom communication, knowing about communication at a practical and theoretical level is not quite the whole picture. You need to be able to implement what you know for maximum impact – and that's where **values** come in.

Values, the things that are important to us, are powerful drivers of emotion and behaviour, and writers like Michael Fullan have shown that the **connection of values to behaviours** is key to school improvement. So, as you start your journey to even better communication skills, take time to:

- Reflect on your values and how you demonstrate them in the classroom
- Communicate your values to your students so that they understand where you are coming from and can predict your reactions to potential actions
- Work with your students on values and learning to make them aware of what is important to *them* about their learning

As you read the reflective summary on the following pages, begin to identify which areas you will focus on first to enhance your communication skills. Find the things that seem to align with your values most and start with these (you will feel motivated to work on these areas). Then challenge yourself to explore areas that you haven't previous considered.

The Moral Imperative of School Leadership by Michael Fullan. Corwin Press, 2003

The what and why of communication

- Develop your communication skills as well as your pedagogy and subject knowledge

- Recognise that communication is a two-way process and the meaning of your communication is the response you get

- Pay attention to all levels of communication: words, voice tone, and body language

- Have an outcome in mind, notice if you are getting it, be flexible and take action

Using words to influence

- There are hidden meanings (or presuppositions) in what is said as well as a surface meaning

- Talk about what you want in the positive rather than mentioning what you don't want

- Use yes sets, connecting words and embedded suggestions

- Use pacing and leading, stories and metaphors to increase effectiveness

Body language and non-verbal communication

- Body language and voice tone in some situations communicate more than words
- Develop your sensory awareness of the body language of others
- Practise and develop key communication postures (such as Levelling) and develop your vocal skills
- Use the space in your classroom to communicate as well as your body language, emotions and learning

Feelings, emotional climate and learning

- Emotions and learning are fundamentally related. The emotional climate you create in your classroom really matters
- Use anchoring to help manage your emotions
- Emotions are contagious. Remember that how you deal with your class affects the next teacher
- Build and develop your one-to-one skills as well as your group presentation skills

Explaining, organising and introducing learning

- Making connections and ensuring attention is important for learning
- Teach pupils about memory and use strategies that support better retention
- Plan learning to illustrate connections and a range of perspectives with approaches such as the Five Steps to Heaven Model
- Be aware of different motivational preferences and ensure that you build expectations during your lessons

Effective questioning

- Good questioning is a key skill in teaching – develop your repertoire of approaches
- Remember that good questions often result in silence as students process their ideas and thoughts (avoid jumping in with the answer)
- Use chunking to challenge thinking and move learning forward
- Incorporate questioning approaches (such as the question square) into your lesson activities

People, mind and brain processes

- Be aware of group processes and how these affect your pupils' behaviour

- Catch your students doing something right to build positive behaviour through a constant process of reward

- Notice psychological preferences. Match these to build motivation and rapport but also challenge your pupils to develop flexibility

- Be aware of your values when you are teaching. Make these explicit and be authentic in relation to your behaviours and their relationship to your values.

Some final thoughts

Excellent communication skills are not a replacement for subject knowledge and sound subject pedagogy. You need to do both to be highly effective as a teacher.

Small changes can often make the biggest difference and require no additional funding to put in place – with communication skills you just do it.

When changing your practice do so as a **reflective practitioner**. Test the effect of things step-by-step and seek feedback from others.

Teaching others is a great way to learn. Use some of the material in this book in training sessions with other teachers and remember to use active learning in the same way that you would with children and teenagers. Learning is, after all, a social process.

Further reading

To find out more about the neuroscience of learning read:
The Learning Brain: Lessons for Education
by Sarah-Jayne Blakemore and Uta Frith.
Blackwell Publishing, 2005
The Brain Book
by Rita Carter.
Dorling Kindersley, 2009

To find out more about NLP influencing and presentation skills for teachers read:
NLP for Teachers: How to be a Highly Effective Teacher by Richard Churches and Roger Terry.
Crown House Publishing, 2007
The NLP Toolkit: Activities and Strategies for Teachers, Trainers and School Leaders
by Roger Terry and Richard Churches.
Crown House Publishing, 2009

To find out more about positive behaviour management read:
Behaviour Management Pocketbook
by Peter Hook and Andy Vass.
Teachers' Pocketbooks, 2011

If you really want to get into influential language and find out about metaphor and storytelling in hypnosis read:
Hypnotic Language: Its Structure and Use
by John Burton and Bob Bodenhamer.
Crown House Publishing, 2000

For an easy to read introduction to organisational behaviour and psychology read:
Psychology and Organizations
by Michael Coates. Heinemann, 2001

To find out more about neuroscience and learning:
Neuroscience and Education: issues and opportunities
A commentary by the Teaching and Learning Research Programme and the Economic and Social Research Council, 2007

Understand the research on teacher effectiveness by reading:
Effective Teaching: evidence and practice
by Dr Daniel Muijs and Prof David Reynolds.
Sage Publications Ltd, 2001